CONTENTS

INTRODUCTION

Thinking of doing a PhD but no one in your family has done one? Then you've come to the right place.

PhDs (and Academia in general) is a whole realm that most people aren't very familiar with. It's not like going to college or trade-school. Most people who go to college or trade-school, or just straight out into the workforce, have some idea about what that path is like, primarily because there are so many people who choose those routes. Usually, their parents chose those routes, so they have people very close to them who can coach them through it.

PhDs, on the other hand, are much rarer. General estimates place around 1-in-75 people have a PhD. Comparing that with those other routes (college, trade-school, and straight out into the workforce), that stat is very low. As such, it is far less common to have direct access to someone with firsthand knowledge of the PhD process, and Academia in general.

If you're in college, you probably have lecturers with PhDs, and so they can provide some semblance of guidance, but in the end, they're usually not that invested in making sure you understand all the ins-and-outs of the PhD process.

So, being someone whose parents, or any other family member, don't have PhDs can make it much harder to understand what a PhD is, let alone why you would want to do one. Those who are the first in their family to enroll in PhD programs are called "first gens", which is short for "first generation PhD student". Other various are "first gener" and "first gen PhD'er".

Often, the driving force behind a first gen wanting to do a PhD is "for a better future", whether that's purely for themselves, or for their family as well. They follow the general conventional wisdom that education will improve your future and career prospects. And that's often the only reason leading them to do a PhD. They simply assume that that wisdom will always hold true, and because there's no level higher than a PhD, getting a PhD will give them the best career possible. That's not always the case. It's still imperative that you understand what a PhD is and what benefits it entails.

A first gen PhD student often lacks an understanding of what a PhD is exactly, what Academia is, and what you have to do during your PhD to get it. This can create many hurdles to overcome, hurdles that non-first gen PhD students don't have. Non-first geners don't have those hurdles simply because they have parents, or even aunts and uncles, whom they can learn from. In fact, many people underestimate the amount they learn about their parents' professions directly from their parents. By virtue that they're just around their parents' work means that they'll naturally absorb some of the knowledge of that field. You can see it for yourself with this simple experiment; think about the fields your parents work in. Now, think about the knowledge you have of it. Now, think about whether you'd have that knowledge if your parents didn't work in that field.

Unknowingly, we absorb a lot of information about our parents' fields. That happens through overhearing general conversations, being in their offices waiting for them, simply seeing a poster on their wall about something in their field, or even through direct conversations with them. And that's where the disadvantage of being a first gen comes from.

Growing up as the daughter or son of someone with a PhD means that you'd have heard of the words, "citations", "papers", "journals", "conferences", "Viva" (or "Defense"), and more. To those who are first gens, those words could have very different meanings to the actual academic ones. For example, is a "citation" something like a speeding ticket from a cop? Isn't a "journal" that thing you write your hopes, dreams, and feelings down in?? What's a "conference"? What do you do there? What's a "Viva", is it like that Ricky Martin song, "Living La Vida Loca", or some kind of revolutionary term, "Viva La Revolucion"?...But to non-first gens, those words already have the academic meanings in their heads.

(If you read those words and didn't know what some of them, or what any of them meant, then you're in the right place. And don't worry, we'll cover them, and more, later on. This book has been designed to not only give overt explanations of various academic terms, but many academic terms are used throughout in a typical manner to help you get used to how you would use them in general conversation. By reading this book you'll pick up many of these words, and how to use them, without having to consciously memorize them.)

We chose those five words because they are so critical to your PhD, and that highlights how "in the dark" many first gens are about the PhD process and Academia in general.

Now that we've introduced what a first generation PhD student is (first gen), the general hurdles in their way, and how they differ to non-first gens, we can now move onto presenting everything you need to know about PhDs and Academia. By the end of this book, you'll understand the PhD process, PhDs, and Academia better than most non-first gens, hence erasing any possible deficit you would have, and even giving you a leg-up. We also end the book with how best to start your PhD – that's something that almost every PhD student struggles with. Once they get into their program, they're faced with the question, "Now what?" The instructions we give in the last sections of the book will kick start your PhD work and will give you very clear direction up to the end of your first year. From there, you'll be in a much better position to plan your own work – everyone needs a little helping hand at the start.

ACADEMIA

The very first topic we need to cover is, Academia. What is Academia? Why is it important? What does it entail?

If you were to look up the word, "Academia" in the dictionary, you'd find a definition along these lines: "the part of society, especially universities, that is connected with studying and thinking, or the activity or job of studying" (Cambridge Dictionary).

Now, that's a nice definition if you already know what Academia is. To those who don't know, it's still not that clear. So, let's go through it more thoroughly and in a way that you can relate to.

If you're reading this book, then chances are that you're at least in the final phases of your Bachelor's degree. You might have finished it already, or even done a Master's.

Think back to when you were sitting in class and there was someone at the front lecturing you about some topic. That person was probably employed by the university, as a lecturer, some kind of professor, or a "teaching assistant". Now, that whole event is part of Academia. You were there learning, your teacher was teaching, and there was thinking going on (hopefully), and the general education process ensued. That's just one part of Academia. But, we can trace the rest of Academia out from this one situation.

Let's consider the material you were learning; where did it come from? It came from someone, somewhere, at some point in time, thinking about it, analyzing it for weaknesses, and finally writing it down for others to learn about. (Now, there could be many people across a long period of time, and that piece of knowledge could've been transferred by several different mediums, but the general process is the same.)

But let's go further back in time; how did that person develop that idea? The most common answer is that, someone paid him/her to do it. In some cases, the person might've been an enthusiast and did it for free, but in most cases that person was paid. So, that's another important aspect of Academia – it relies on money. The technical term for money in Academia is, "Funding". You don't say you get money from the Government to carry out research, you get "Funding" from the Government. It's essentially the same thing. The word "Funding" is simply preferred because the connotations of "Funding" is different to "Money".

So, we now know that that piece of knowledge you learnt in class came from someone, somewhere, and was transferred through some kind of medium to you. We also know that that person was likely paid to find out that information through funding. But, one question still remains; why? Why did s/he research it in the first place?

The simple answer is that s/he was probably told to, and in return s/he got money and/or a qualification (like a PhD!). Now, we could circle back and say that, s/he was told to because the employer (usually the university) got money (we mean, "funding") to do the research. And the person/company/Government who gave that funding wanted the answer. In some cases, that piece of knowledge might make a direct impact; for example, the company might use that knowledge to help improve a process and make more money, or gain a competitive advantage. In other cases, that piece of knowledge doesn't make an immediate, or a direct, impact on anything. For example, Leonardo Da Vinci invented many different inventions that weren't possible until recently (in fact, many of those inventions still aren't possible with our level of technology, and perhaps they won't be until far in the future), but the research is carried out because someone, somewhere convinced someone with money that they should fund the research.

We've now covered the two general halves of Academia; the research side, and the dissemination side. They interlock. You've already had experience with the dissemination side, where you sat in class and learnt during your Bachelor's. But, you've probably had very limited exposure to the research side. And that side is where the PhD process predominantly lives.

You can think of the research side as effectively like a consultancy – people/companies/Governments come to the university and ask it to conduct research, or the university goes around to people/companies/Governments and tries to convince them that they should fund a particular research project.

Roles And Positions In The University

Now, we've covered a lot about the research side, and we need to unpack it a little more to explain the various positions and roles; we said that the university goes around to get funding for a project, but that's not quite clear – a university can't do anything, it's an inanimate object. More precisely, someone inside the university goes around to get funding. The university, in effect, is an amalgamation of various people, from professors, to deans, to presidents and chancellors, to admins, to PhD students, and more. Each group has their own role to play, and without one of those roles, the university will severely stumble, or even fail.

We won't go into each role in detail; we'll cover these roles, but focus more in detail on those ones that are specifically intertwined with PhD students – the people who will greatly affect your PhD.

PhD students are the workhorses. They do the research, and effectively all of the intellectual menial roles that no one else does. For example, they could also be required to do marking or assisting in lectures – the things that no one else either wants to do or is qualified to do (for example, a technician isn't qualified to mark, but a professor is. But a professor often doesn't want to because they've got bigger fish to fry, so that task often falls to PhD students).

Professors are the ones who run research groups. They're effectively organizers. Ideally, they've got a lot of knowledge about all the different aspects of conducting research, from the general techniques, to how to get funding, to how to present the work so that it's good for the university's image, to directing the group towards the research that is relevant, to hiring the right people. Within the research group you can find the various levels of researchers, from Master's students and PhD students, to postdocs, to "PI's". There are two new terms there that we haven't covered.

A "postdoc" (which is short for, "postdoctoral researcher") is some who has finished a PhD and is now just researching. Some postdoc positions are little more than PhD positions (without the award at the end), but some are genuinely big steps up in responsibility, including getting grant money (funding), and conducting their own research without much input from anyone higher up.

A "PI" (which is short for, "principal investigator") is the person who, as the name suggests, is the principal investigator of the project. That means that that person is generally the one who calls the shots when it comes to how things are done – how the data is processed, what data will be written up and disseminated, and what the funding will be spent on. Sometimes, the PI is also the one who got the grant money in the first place. A PI can also be a professor, but not necessarily. Sometimes, the professor is one above that and oversees a few different PIs.

Generally speaking, the rungs on the ladder of research positions (from lowest to highest) are: Master's student, PhD student, postdoc, PI, professor. Any step above that and you're no longer in the research group, but more of an upper manager, for example a dean, president, a chancellor.

As a PhD student, you can have a multitude of different supervisors (supervisors are those people who direct your work, and your PhD progress). You might have a PI, professor, and even a postdoc. Each one will have their role. For example, postdocs often play the role of the competent researchers. They know what they're doing and they're often the ones who directly help PhD students do their research. Kind of like a big brother or sister. The higher up the ladder a supervisor is, the less hands-on they'll be with helping you – you don't usually have a professor crunching data or preparing the test specimens, but you do often get a postdoc doing that.

What are the roles of PI's and professors as supervisors? In essence, they're usually more helpful from the logistical side of things. They can throw their weight around to get enough resources, and organize things for you. Say that you need to get something approved by the university, that's where their expertise comes in handy – they've likely done all of that bureaucratic stuff before, so they can guide you and even push things through quicker. The better a PI or professor they are, the more they can help you.

So, we can really divide a research group into two extremes. The technical extreme and the administrative extreme. PhD students, Master's students, and postdocs usually fall on the more technical side, while PI's and professors usually fall on the more administrative side.

Any higher than the typical professor results in an upper management role. These include roles such as the dean, chancellor, and president.

Deans typically oversee many research groups, and even all the research groups in the entire university. For example, your university might have a dean of research (who would oversee all research), or it might have several deans, for example, the dean of physical sciences – someone who's in charge of all the research that goes on in just the physical sciences faculty. It just depends on the university.

Chancellors and presidents are the head honchos. They're usually highly connected, industrially, politically, and in any other way you can think of. There are several other positions in between the deans and professors, but they're not really that important for the typical PhD student to understand.

How Your PhD Fits Into The University

We've covered the general structure of Academia, so now it's time to explain how your PhD, and PhDs in general, fit into it.

We categorized a university into two main halves. Dissemination of knowledge, and the finding of that knowledge. Arguably, the latter is more important than the former; if you don't have any knowledge to disseminate then you can't disseminate anything of value. And the more groundbreaking the knowledge is, the greater the demand for that knowledge is, thereby increasing the demand for its dissemination.

We also covered that the people who generally do the research in a university (those who find the knowledge) are PhD students. There are several sources out there giving figures for how much of the research at a university is conducted by PhD students, but the general range is between 50% and 80%. In other words, the majority of the research is done by PhD students, and that's where your PhD fits in.

Your PhD is so important to the proper functioning of the university. Without PhD students, the majority of the research done will disappear. If there's very little knowledge being found, then the dissemination side of the university also greatly suffers. So, PhD students are an integral part of the university, and without them it could not function. That's not to say that they're the lynchpin; there are many other positions that are equally important. For example, without those who get the grant money to conduct the research (PI's, postdocs, and professors, and in some cases the PhD students themselves), the research would not go ahead either; even if a PhD student were willing to work for free, they wouldn't have the resources needed.

So, you can see how vital your PhD is to the university, but also how it fits into a greater network of roles and functions, with many of them also being vital.

This is also a good point to highlight that Bachelor's and Master's students are also usually vital parts of the university; the money brought in by tuition paying students is often a necessary portion of the university's overall funding, and we've seen that over the last few years where the number of Bachelor's and Master's students in the U.S.A. has dropped and as a result many universities are foreclosing or predicting foreclosure in the not too distant future.

So, along with several other roles, your role as a PhD student is highly important, not just in the direct way that it produces knowledge, but in the following indirect ways:

-Increases the knowledge base for dissemination

-Makes the university more attractive to prospective students

-Makes the university more attractive to prospective funders

We've already covered the first indirect way, let's move onto the second way, making the university more attractive to prospective students; universities are ranked. In fact, there are several different rankings that you can look a university up in. The three main international ones are, the "Times Higher Education World University Rankings", the "Shang Hai Academic Ranking of World Universities", and the "QS World University Rankings". Each of these can be easily found on the net. There are many other rankings, but these are the most highly regarded, and as such, they hold a lot of weight over the perceived quality of a particular university. As such, a university that is ranked higher will generally enjoy a greater demand from prospective students. The greater the the demand, the more a university can charge for tuition, and thereby continue to grow.

The third indirect way a PhD student benefits the university, by making it more attractive to prospective funders, occurs because the more competent the researchers are, the more a funder will want to have their research done by those researchers; these funders often don't like throwing money away, so they want to get as much bang for their buck as possible.

As a side note, there are some funders who almost specialize in wasting money. It might seem hard to believe, but one such funder is the Government. Much of the money a Government invests into research is wasted, but that's from the point of view of wanting research to happen. You see, the Government isn't always interested in having research done, in fact, much of the time it's more interested in employment, and by throwing a few bucks around they make sure that people have jobs. So, the research that's done is beside the point.

Academic Rankings

We covered in the last section that there's an array of university rankings, and there are three major ones in the world that people frequently consult. In order for you to more fully understand how the Academic system works, you need to understand how these rankings work.

How is knowing how these ranking systems work important for your PhD?

Simply because you'll better understand the pressures placed on you, why they're being placed on you, and how best to alleviate them as a PhD student. Yes, PhD students also have deadlines, requirements, and goals to fulfil, and much of the time these stressors stem directly from the university system – you'll understand this a little more after this section. So, let's explain how the rankings work.

Around the world, there are thousands of universities. It might seem surprising because many people only really hear about a few elite ones and the ones in their home state, but if you think about it, it's logical that there are so many universities. Hundreds in the USA, hundreds in Europe, Asia, South America, and so on. The various international university ranking systems rank most of these – generally the top thousand or so.

The metrics by which these universities are judged and ranked are diverse, but the general metrics are as follows:

1) "Employability" of students once graduated

2) Amount of research outputted

3) Quality of research outputted

4) Level of diversity of students

5) Level of funding

Depending on the ranking system, there are other metrics, but these ones above are the most common, widespread, and important.

By looking at these five metrics, it is obvious that three of them are directly related to research (metrics 2, 3, and 5). The other two metrics are indirect, but are still greatly impacted by the research side of the university; the "employability" of graduated students depends on a lot of things, and one of those things is the knowledge base of the university. For example, it's not uncommon for Bachelor's and Master's courses to utilize some of the labs or resources that the researchers have built and gotten funding for. As a result, these labs and resources greatly improve the quality of the graduates.

The level of diversity of students is also impacted by the research side of the university. The better, and the more, research a university puts out, the better it is perceived to be. There's a reason why Harvard gave birth to Facebook, <u>even though the founder didn't even graduate</u>. Furthermore, the better, and more, research outputted, the better a university will score in metrics 2 and 3, which will increase their world ranking, which will attract more students (metric 4).

The above discussion is just a brief one describing how the rankings are calculated. You could go much deeper into them, and into each one individually, but right now, you don't need to know too much more about them. One reason for that is, each university values one or two of the ranking systems more than any of the others. For example, your university might value the Times Higher Ed one the most and not really care about the others. Why? For several reasons; it could be because their particular fields only focus on that one, or their funders focus on that one, etc. Having said that, as said before, all of the rankings have the same general metrics that they rank each university by, it's just the minor details that change. If you want to know more about a specific ranking system, simply Google it and you will quickly find how much they value each metric.

Now that we've covered what influences the various university rankings, we come to the part about how the rankings are important for PhD students.

Look at those five general metrics, you can probably deduce how your research, being a PhD student, impacts all of them. We've already touch upon how, but let's go further, and in particular, let's look at the second and third metrics closer.

The second and third metrics are quite simple – quantity and quality...but what do you mean by quantity? Quantity of what? Research and findings aren't physical, it's not like you can say, "I got 3 feet and 3 inches of research done this year!" Furthermore, how do you measure the quality of research? So, the question becomes, how do you measure the quantity and quality of someone's research?

Academia has actually devised a very simple method, you can sum it up in one word: "Papers!" That's right, papers. You might not know what "papers" mean? In a nutshell, a paper is a document that you detail your research in, then get it "published" in a "journal".

Now, there were a lot of new words in that last paragraph, so let's break it down into plain English: you write your research up into a document (a paper, aka "manuscript" or "article"). You then send it off to an organization (called a "journal"), who then assess it for its quality. If they deem it to be of the standard they're looking for, then they'll put it on their website and in their magazine for all to find (They "publish it").

There are more journals than you can imagine. There are journals for everything, from geology, to physics, to English, to even how to eat an ice cream properly (maybe not that last one, <u>but</u> there are definitely journals out there that will publish papers to do with how to eat ice cream properly, and that's not a joke). As a side note before moving on, you should be careful of a branch of journals known as "predatory journals". This is an overarching term applied to all the journals that have questionable publishing practices. This could involve charging you significant sums of money to publish, to taking your research and publishing it themselves, to taking money and not even publishing. There are several organizations that try to collate a list of these journals, however, sometimes they get it wrong – some journals that are predatory aren't on there, and some that are on those lists aren't predatory. But don't worry, that's what your supervisors are there for! Use their knowledge and judgement to navigate these journals.

Let's get back onto the topic at hand – the quantity and quality of your research output; we've now figured out that you can assess the quantity of your research by the simple idea of a paper. Five papers is more research than four, and less than six (strictly speaking, that's not always the case, but it's usually what everyone assumes, and for all intensive purposes, that's the system we use). And that's what universities are after, more papers! In fact, it's gotten so dire that almost everyone's career in Academia is governed by the number of papers they output. It's led to a saying, "publish or perish", whereby if you don't publish, then you won't get promoted, or even have your contract renewed. The reason why you need to publish is because that increases the university rankings and the general reputation of the university to funders. That has had a massive knockdown effect onto PhD students.

Remember when we said that the majority of the research conducted by a university is done by PhD students? Well, that means that PhD students have a direct effect on the university's funding and its reputation. As a result, almost every university in the top 200 in the world has put in a requirement that a PhD student needs a particular number of papers, and the rest of the universities around the world are copying suit. 20 years ago, such a thing was almost unheard of, now, it's commonplace. That number changes from university to university, with some requiring only one, while others require eight. So, you can easily see how these rankings and the lust for more papers directly impacts PhD students, and yourself.

So, a very simple, but difficult, requirement has now been placed on PhD students. In order to graduation, you will need to have published a certain number of papers.

We've now covered how this academic system impacts your PhD with the quantity of research you need to do, and why. Let's now move onto the quality aspect.

How do you measure the quality of research? Do two researchers get in a room, and each one says, "My research is better", and the last one standing wins? Sometimes that pretty much happens :). But, there's a more widespread way, and it pivots off of papers.

To understand how to quantify the quality of research, we first have to understand another metric in the "world of papers".

First, let's ask the following question: why do research?

Inevitably, the answer will consist, at least partly, of the fact that it should help society. What's more, no one's research is ever standalone. There is always a whole field behind it that it's working from. And your papers will also get included in this field soon enough. When that happens, people from around the world will read your papers and use its contents to help them with their research – you might find something out that greatly helps another researcher. Now, when they write their paper, they'll "cite" your paper. What that means is, the research is effectively saying, "This person did this research and it impacted my work in such a way". This is called "citing".

The more citations a paper has (the more times people cite your paper), the more influential it is. And the more influential it is, the more highly regarded it is. Now, that logic is not strictly true because sometimes you get a very highly cited paper, but many of those citations are from papers that are disproving something that it documented. But, that weakness in the system of citations is usually overlooked. (No one ever said that Academia was fastidious.)

So, we now have a way of measuring the quality of a paper – how many citations it gets, and those citations are usually counted within certain timeframes. You could quote the 2-year citation index, the 3-year, 5-year, or quote the total number of citations it has had over its entire lifetime. The goal is to compare the same timeframes among the various papers.

That's how the quality of your research will largely be determined.

What does that mean for you as a PhD student? It means that you'll be limited to a particular set of journals. Universities want as high a quality of research as possible, so they'll say that you can't publish in "that" journal because its citation index isn't high enough, but another one is. Let's cover quickly how to differentiate the quality of various journals. It's quite simple, you count how many citations the various papers published by the journals have over a certain time interval, and average. For example, if a journal published 13 papers in its February 2013 issue, and in total all of those papers received 65 citations within 3 years (up until February 2016), then the average citation index for each paper is, 65/13 = 5.0. From there, you can compare journals. Which time interval you use is up to you. Now, this number is called the "Impact Factor". It's an important term, so make sure to remember it. A journal with an impact factor of 3.2 is better than a journal with an impact factor of 2.0. (Once again, that's not strictly true for a number of reasons, but that's what every agrees upon.)

What does that mean for you as a PhD student? How does that affect you?

It makes your PhD harder. That's the plain truth. The higher the citation index of a journal (the higher it's impact factor), the more people will want to have their papers published in it, which creates more competition because the journal only has a limited number of spots per month, and so they can be more fussy.

In the short run, it's worse for you, but in the long run, it's not such a bad thing; if you publish in a better journal (that's to say, a journal with a higher Impact Factor), you'll generally get more citations. The main reason is because everyone believes that the work must be better because it was published in a great journal, so they can trust it more. We've already seen one way in which the number of citations you get is not necessarily linked to quality (if people are citing your work because they're disproving it), but as we've said, people generally overlook that. The fact that they believe that your paper is better will naturally lead to more citations. The more citations you get, the better your chances of getting promoted in Academia…and the rat race continues!

The final point to discuss about papers is the publication process. Once you send your paper off to the journal, a few things happen. The first is that the editor of the journal (effectively, the boss of the journal) will do a quick scan to see what topic it's on, where it's from, and the general quality. If your work fits the journal and the quality is good, then the editor will move it onto the next phase, which is called "peer review".

This next stage is exactly what it sounds like, your peers review your work; the editor finds a few people, hopefully in your field, to read your paper and make comments about its quality. From there, three general possibilities exist; 1) your paper is accepted immediately, 2) your paper is sent back to you with comments for you to revise and incorporate into your paper, and then re-submit the paper, 3) your paper is rejected. Everyone gets papers rejected. So, don't take it personally. You could get papers rejected for a multitude of reasons. The first reason is that it genuinely isn't of a high enough standard. The second reason is that the editor/peer reviewers didn't understand its value. The third reason is that your topic isn't quite in vogue – yes, Academia has fashion as well, for example, when COVID-19 hit, so many people suddenly wrote papers about it just to get them published, even if they didn't work in that field!

While the impact factor of a journal is important, other factors are equally important for you. Let's give you an example. Say you have two journals, one journal has a 3-year impact factor of 3.5, the other has a 3-year impact factor of 2.0. You might be tempted to immediately pick the first one because its impact factor is much better. However, there are other factors to consider. These include, how easy it is to get published, how long it will take, and how good the reviewers are; if it's 10 times harder to get published in the first journal, then the pay off probably won't be as high as giving it to the second journal and putting more effort into more research to make more papers. If it will take 2 years to get published in the first journal and only 6 months in the second journal, then that could greatly delay your PhD completion (if you have to publish a certain number of papers before you finish, then you can't finish until you've published those papers). If the journal has terrible reviewers, then that will greatly increase the chances of your paper being rejected, not to mention all the head-aches it will cause. There's one resource out there that has tackled these issues, and other ones. It's called the "Journal Rater" by an organization called "PhD Voice". It's a database freely accessible to everyone where you can rate your experiences with journals on a whole host of important factors. You can also look up journals to see what the experience of others are with them. From this groundbreaking tool, you can much better select the best journal for your work. You can find it here, https://phdvoice.org/journalrater/.

We've now covered Academia, it's underlying principles, and how that affects you as a PhD student, let's move onto what a PhD is.

WHAT IS A PHD?

A PhD stands for "Doctor of Philosophy"...okay, but that doesn't really tell us much. (As a side note, you almost certainly know that someone with a PhD is entitled to use the title "Dr" in front of their name. What's more, you've probably heard a bunch of times someone saying that someone with a PhD isn't really a doctor. Well, you should know that that's false. In fact, someone with a PhD is far more of a doctor than a medical doctor is; the title "doctor" has been used for someone with a PhD about 200 years longer than someone with a medical degree. The medical doctors borrowed the title from PhD holders about 100 years ago to lend themselves the credibility that PhD holders have – and the credibility that you'll have. So, in fact, when someone says that someone with a PhD isn't a real doctor, they don't know what they're talking about. Back to what a PhD is...)

So, a Doctor of Philosophy. What does that mean. In essence, a Doctor of Philosophy is someone who is an expert in a particular field. Now, for most PhDs, research of some kind is involved, and for those types of PhD holders, they're also experts in how to research. Being able to research effectively isn't as easy as one might think. Your analytical skills improve dramatically during a PhD and even to the point where you can quite accurately assess the information of an entirely different field. Those analytical skills are highly transferable, and to a large extent, a PhD is an exercise in dramatically improving them.

When you come across someone with a PhD, you can be fairly confident that that person is analytical and can assess information for its veracity. That's not to say that every PhD holder is as competent as the next, but they're all at a certain level and that level is significantly higher than the average person without a PhD.

For those few subjects that don't involve much research, you'll still be an expert in that field, and your analytical skills will still be much sharper than someone who hasn't done a PhD, but you won't be as well versed in conducting research, but you'll pick up different skills.

Let's cover what being analytical means.

In a nutshell, analytical means being logical, thorough, rigorous, and contentious. That means that when a certain situation arises, you'll calmly go through each possibility, think deeply about each one, then do your best to weigh up the pros and cons of each possibility before making any decisions or plans.

Let's now cover what research is.

We said before that research isn't as straightforward as some people might think. Research hinges on being analytical, but it also hinges on being precise and accurate with your focus. For example, one of the greatest difficulties that many early PhD students have is being able to define the thrust of their project. Let me give you an example, say that you want to research some like the benefits of a new food source on Goldfish (something that everyone can understand). It sounds like a fairly straightforward project, until you start digging deeper; off the top of our heads, we can rattle off the following questions:

-What do you mean by benefits? Is that health benefits in general? One particular health benefit, such as the shine of their skin? Is that to do with the reduction of the toxicity of their waste products and the resulting healthier bowl water? Is that to do with the digestibility of the food? Is that to do with the general balance of the nutrients in the food? Is it some other kind of benefits than health benefits?

-What timescale are we looking at? Some foods are very good in small irregular doses, others are better in consistent and regular doses.

-Does the amount of food you give them factor into the project?

And so you can see a whole bunch of questions on a project that seems so mundane to begin with. And that's what we mean by having a very precise and accurate research project. A much better research project would be something like the following: my project focuses on determining the effects of this particular food on the toxicity of the waste products of the Goldfish that consume it exclusively. In particular, the waste product is ammonia.

That research project just defined is quite "tight" – it's precise and accurate. There aren't too many avenues that could be pursed, ergo, everyone will understand exactly what you're investigating.

From that simple example, you can see how tricky research can be. But don't worry, research is like riding a bicycle – once you learn the system, you never forget. We'll cover how to do research effectively later on in the, "What Do You Do In A PhD" chapter.

One thing that many people don't realize is that, a PhD is not about creativity – in the perfect world, it would be, but in the real world it's most definitely not.

In the perfect world, you'd get creative and think about all sorts of possibilities and whether they'd be possible. In the real world, that's rarely the case. One of the major reasons why the vast majority of PhD students don't get creative is because they're scared. In Academia, there's a very strong phenomenon called the "Imposter Syndrome". It's effectively where you don't feel confident about your work. It has become so ingrained that it's almost a cult-like religion and because people talk about it so much, it becomes a perpetual cycle that people get caught up in.

That feeling of not having confidence in your work or your abilities shuts down your ability to think creatively. You get scared to step out of the box and think about things that others haven't thought about for fear of looking incompetent. I, John, can tell you firsthand that when you start talking about possibilities that no one has thought about, you get called a lot of names, you even get laughed at…until those ideas are proven right. Then people develop this mix of resentment (because you're smarter than they are, so they feel incompetent) and awe. That leads to a very complex situation, but you don't need to worry about that so early in your PhD life. (If you want to get a good idea about what people in Academia are like, watch the movie "Good Will Hunting" – there's a scene in it where the main character, Will, a young, brash, but genius guy, outsmarts a professor in Mathematics. The professor is immediately broken because he can't believe that he was outsmarted by someone, especially someone so young. He pinned his entire self-worth to being the smartest person.)

If you play your cards right, your creativity will go through the roof during your PhD, and you should definitely nurture it. There's nothing wrong with being wrong. At the end of the day, **Academia is just one massive exercise is being a little less wrong each day.** The more wrong you are, the more you find the limits of your field. Remember, the more creative you are, the more innovative you are and the greater the impact you'll have. Don't let your creativity get snuffed out by what other people think, especially not during your PhD – your PhD is a period in your life where you're just there to learn.

WHY WOULD YOU WANT TO DO A PHD?

Being a first gen, the benefits of doing a PhD may not be what you think. Let's go through some of the reasons we've heard. These reasons are from first gens:

-"I want to make bank."

-"I want to make a better life for me and my family."

-"I want the title."

These are all things that we've heard prospective, or early, PhD students say, verbatim. Unfortunately, only one out of those three are literally true, and even that one doesn't entail the benefits that you might think.

Before going further, we should stress that the underlying factor determining whether those three things are true or not is location. In countries that have a very strong social class structure, all of these things are true. For example, I, Neil, worked in the Middle East for a few years. In that environment, the class structure was very strong – everyone had their place and it was rare to mix with people who weren't in your class. Being a PhD holder, a proper Doctor, put you in a very high class. People respected you simply because of your title. In fact, I threw my title around a few times to get out of fines and get treated better – it was normal. Someone who didn't have that title couldn't do that because they were in a lower class. That title, in those highly stratified social class environments, will mean that you will "make bank", you will "make a better life for yourself and your family", and you will obviously have that title and the respect that goes with it. The wheels of bureaucracy turn much easier, and attributing your name to something (with the "Dr" in front of it of course) will automatically make it much more successful.

In the West, the social class system fell by the wayside long ago and that means that currently the title Doctor gives you almost no advantages. You won't "make bank", and you probably won't even have a better life; most people who have PhDs will tell you that they work very long hours, have poor family lives, and they are more likely to suffer health problems than most other professions.

It's surprising how many PhD students do a PhD because of those reasons above but don't realize that, in the West, those goals won't be fulfilled. People whose parents have PhDs more readily understand that having a PhD won't lead you to "the promised land". The reason why they are less likely to believe in those points above is because they see that their parents don't make huge sums of money, etc.

Having covered that a PhD won't lead you to those benefits above, the next question is, what will a PhD lead you to?

From a social point of view, a PhD will simply allow you to work in particular fields. But remember that those fields won't be any more lucrative, generally speaking. It simply means that you'll be able to do a certain kind of work, and that kind of work is usually less physically exhausting than other jobs. Not too long ago, we were talking with an academic and he said that he did an 11 hour day working with his father doing general labor. He also said that he'll never complain about academic work again! Sitting in a chair and writing most of the day isn't that strenuous. And that's really all a PhD will give you straight up, from a career point of view. But you get far more from a PhD than that, if you allow it.

One of the most overlooked benefits of doing a PhD is a personal one. If you approach a PhD with a mindset of wanting to learn, then you'll develop many valuable skills along the way. Some of these skills include, better reasoning and analytical abilities, better writing skills, better forethought, and a greater objectivity. While all of those skills will almost always help you perform your job well (whatever that job may be), it won't really be accompanied with a higher salary. However, that doesn't mean that you shouldn't be ecstatic about being better in all those ways.

Let's give you an example; over the past few years (2016 to 2020), a lot has gone on in the world from the MeToo Movement, to Fake News, to Donald Trump being elected, to Greta Thunberg being in everyone's face, to the Black Lives Matter Movement, to COVID-19, and more. Everything you hear is an opinion. "Fake News" taught us that, where two news outlets contradict each other. The typical person gets caught up in all of the information forced upon them, regardless of whether that information is correct or incorrect – they can't discern the correct from the incorrect very easily (note that that's on average). The average person has thought that the world was going to come to an end more times in the last 4 years than in the last 20. What people need in order to wade through all of this information, to discern the correct information from the nonsense, is reasoning ability. That's exactly what you develop during your PhD. When everyone was running around buying toilet paper during COVID-19, the reasonable person would've realized that food is a much higher priority, after all, if you don't have food, then you won't need toilet paper... In a nutshell, the ability to reason helps you become more immune to hysteria and false information. That might not seem like a lot to some people, but that's the difference between being an independent thinker and being a robot.

In addition to those skills you develop, another major attraction to doing a PhD is that you have the chance to improve the world. Again, that might not be very attractive to some, with those people simply interested in themselves and what they gain out of it, but we'll get to that in a little while. For those who genuinely want to make the world better, a PhD gives you the chance to do so; you can research a topic that lies close to your heart and by helping the community understand it better (through your research), the problem can be better dealt with, or living conditions can be improved, and so on. It's a highly rewarding feeling to see your research spawning a new field and having that field become popular (it takes some years, but if you're patient, you'll see it too).

Now for those people who are only interested in the reward they'll receive, well there's a kicker to improving the world. Those people who want rewards are usually after it in the form of money. Let us, once again, tell you that that's not going to happen in Academia. But, it can happen out in the real world. The difference being, that you need to focus on the value you're giving other people, and that ties in with your PhD and research; the more value your results give, the better position you're in to capitalize on it. You might think that that's far-fetched, to go into business from your PhD research. It only is because most people don't do it. But, I, Neil, did just that. I used what I learnt in my PhD to springboard into a business. Let me tell you that, business hinges on how much value you can give to someone in return for their money. So, you can make money out of your PhD, but you usually have to leave Academia to do so. The more value you create through your work during your PhD, the more you can capitalize on it post-PhD. And the more ideas you get during your PhD, and the more you learn, the more fuel you have to make it successful.

In reality, a PhD is one big exercise in being original. Nothing creates success like being original.

The Title And Job Prospects

Another benefit of having a PhD is the title, but it's a double-edged sword. You're probably already aware of the general receptions to someone with a PhD. They range from warm to frosty; some people will be very pleased to mix with someone with a PhD (your mother, for example, will be very proud that her son/daughter has a PhD, and will probably mention it any chance she gets). On the other hand, some people aren't so thrilled to know that you've got a PhD; some of your pre-PhD friends will probably be less than excited to mix with you anymore.

One of the highly counter-intuitive results of having a PhD is that, it will probably be harder for you to get a job. Yes, that's right. It will actually be harder. Let's clarify; for some roles, having a PhD is almost mandatory. For example, if you want to work as a chemical engineer researching the latest vaccines, then a PhD is highly helpful to getting that job. However, there's a class of jobs where having a PhD will significantly reduce your chances of getting hired. We call this class of jobs the "Hostile Jobs". What do we mean by that term? Well, in essence, they're jobs where your simple presence will make your coworkers feel threatened. As a result, there will be much hostility towards you.

What kind of jobs classify as "Hostile Jobs"? There are a few different types. Firstly, a job where your immediate boss doesn't have a PhD will often be a Hostile Job. The reason is because, they'll feel threatened by the fact that you're more educated than they are and so they will feel that their job is at risk – they might get fired and you'll take their place, or you might leap-frog them and become their boss. If you ever apply to that kind of job, it is almost certain that you won't get it – the boss will make sure that you're seen as not right for the job, even if you're perfect.

Another type of Hostile Job is the one where your peers don't have PhDs. To give you an idea of this kind of environment, imagine working in a place and all of a sudden someone 5 years younger than you and with a PhD walks in. How would you feel? Probably fairly insecure. And that's exactly how your coworkers will feel. As a result, they become very hostile towards you. Now, you're far more likely to get that job than the one where your potential boss doesn't have a PhD, but it won't be a very good one.

In reality, the only jobs that are well suited to someone with a PhD are the ones where your immediate peers have a similar qualification. That creates an interesting dilemma; when you finish your PhD and start looking for jobs, you'll obviously find those jobs where having a PhD is mandatory, but there will be far more jobs that don't *need* a PhD but it is still desirable to have one. The catch here is that those jobs often prioritize experience over qualifications. So, being fresh out of grad school will mean that most potential employers will see you as having almost no experience (unless you had a job beforehand). This is actually wrong – doing a PhD means that you've got at least a few years of experience managing your own project, and even other people, but because most people don't even know what a PhD entails, that experience won't count during a job application. So, experience-wise, you're now on the same level as someone with a Bachelor's or Master's degree. The only real advantage you have is in the qualification area. As a result, you might think that you'll be more readily hired than those with only Bachelor's and Master's degrees, but then you have the problem where your boss won't have a PhD, and so they won't want to hire you because you're a threat – it's a very convoluted and illogical situation, but that's how it is.

Now, if you manage to get a job where your peers don't have PhDs, then that won't be very good either – you'll be public enemy number one and no one will help you learn the ropes of the job. It's their way of mitigating the perceived risk you pose to their careers.

From that short description above it doesn't seem like a great idea to get a PhD...at least when it comes to your career. But it's not all bad. While getting a PhD might seem like you're limiting your employment options, it's more accurate to say that getting a PhD changes your employment options; while those Hostile Jobs will be largely off the table, a new set of jobs will come onto the table. We mentioned earlier that a PhD is actually great training for starting your own business. Most people don't realize that because Academia is very cushy – they observe their supervisors and professors and see that many of them literally can't get fired (unless they break the code of conduct) – they have jobs for life. But, there are key characteristics of the PhD life that transfer incredibly well to entrepreneurship. Here's a short list with some of the more important skills:

-   Ability to work under pressure
-   Ability to handle uncertainty
-   Ability to work long hours without much reward
-   Ability to work to deadlines
-   Ability to communicate succinctly
-   Ability to live on a very small income

Each of the skills in the list above are imperative for a business owner to have. And each one of them will be tested and grown during your PhD – trust us! If you don't believe us, then ask any PhD student if their ability in any of those areas has been tested and improved during their PhD!

Now, we won't go through how each of these abilities are tested and improved during your PhD in this section. We'll leave it for a general explanation in the next section. But, let's go into how each of these abilities helps an entrepreneur.

The first one is to work under pressure. Unlike a regular job, being a business owner is filled with pressures. You have pressures from all side, from lack of time, to lack of money, to lack of work-force, and so on. Things that you didn't even think of will pop up and create pressures that you didn't even know could exist. But, the increased tolerance to pressure, which was developed during your PhD, will put you in good stead.

Being a business owner is almost the definition of uncertainty. While regular employees are almost guaranteed their next pay-check (and even the next year's worth of pay), a business owner isn't guaranteed tomorrow's. What's more, they're not guaranteed customers or innovation, or anything really. Being able to handle uncertainty is key to being a business owner. And guess what? If you've done a PhD, then you'll have that ability in spades!

PhD students often work long hours, and they don't often get rewarded for it. That works right into the business owner's wheelhouse – you might spend months on an idea only for it to flop. And that's just how it is. You have to dust yourself off and try something else, and with just as much conviction and gusto as you did the first time. PhD students, and holders, are good at that.

Many deadlines are placed on PhD students. You'll often have a bunch of deadlines for all different things. You'll need to juggle them and make sure you meet them. That sounds like a skill a business owner needs!

We haven't covered what you do during a PhD yet (that's to come in the next chapter), but suffice it to say that, a PhD student does years of work, and will have to be able to concisely communicate it in a dissertation, in a presentation, or in an "elevator pitch". It's hard, but you develop that skill. And business owners need the same skill – you need to communicate your ideas succinctly and clearly to potential stakeholders, customers, and employees. Yet another crucial skill you learn during your PhD that is directly transferable to entrepreneurship.

Finally, PhD students live with very little income. Many of them actually experience a reduction in the quality of their life when they begin – having to live with many other people, eating ramen and spaghetti every night, using the university's internet connection to do the more data intense things in life (like downloading movies or playing video games with your friends), and so... Well, as an entrepreneur starting out, you'll also be heavily cash-strapped and once again that skill you learnt during your PhD will be vital.

So, it's clear that one of the career opportunities that doing a PhD actually makes more likely is entrepreneurship. That's all well and good, but what if you don't want to own your own business? Well, firstly, around 97% of Americans say that they'd like to work for themselves – so, doing a PhD is perfect, but for those 3% who don't, there's Academia (as well as "think-tank" organizations).

As we've covered, Academia involves universities, professors, lecturers, and so on. Doing a PhD is becoming more and more mandatory in order to become a professor. The better the university, the more likely you'll need to have a PhD to even become a lecturer.

Let's briefly go through the general roles that you could be hired for.

For people with PhDs, there are two general roles that you can be hired for, researching or teaching. Again, the same two general areas that we went through earlier.

When you're first starting out (just after your PhD), you can be hired as a number of things; a post-doc, a TA, an assistant professor, a general researcher. Let's go through each of these items.

A post-doc: we've already covered this position, so let's just go through it briefly again. A post-doc is simply someone who is doing more research after their PhD. They are often involved in planning and conducting the research, as well as getting grant money (convincing someone, somewhere to give them money to do research in a particular area). Post-docs can sometimes teach as well, but it isn't that common.

A TA (teaching-assistant) is exactly what it sounds like – it's someone who assists in teaching. That could be actually doing most of the lectures, or simply just the background work, like marking, preparing the lectures, or handling the admin side of the class. A TA almost never does any research as part of their role.

An assistant professor is someone who can do anything from almost exclusively teaching to exclusively researching. They're one rung up the ladder to post-docs and TA's, so they're usually more involved with the management of the research or teaching. They can also do a little of both. Now, there are two types of assistant professors; tenure-track and non-tenure-track. Tenure is where the university employs you for life. Only under very extreme circumstances (such as a severe lack of funding, or you doing something illegal or immoral) can you be fired. It can be very cushy. An assistant professor who is tenure-tracked means that they're working towards becoming tenured. Along that track they need to fulfil various criteria such as publish a certain number of papers, or get a certain amount of funding, etc. A non-tenure-track assistant professor isn't working towards tenure, but is simply working a job. After assistant professor, the next step is associate professor, and then finally professor (emeritus professor is the last stage, but an emeritus professor is not as prominent as a professor simply because they're semi-retired).

Finally, you could be hired in academia as a general researcher. The line between post-doc and general researcher is blurry and each university has their own definitions, but in essence they're almost the same thing. Perhaps, the post-doc has certain criteria to fulfil, like publishing a certain number of papers by the end, but it varies from university to university, and even professor to professor.

A final thing you should be aware of is that, approximately 3% of PhD graduates become professors.

We mentioned earlier something about "think-tank" organizations. Many PhD graduates get jobs in companies that are heavily involved in R&D (research & development). That is a very likely career for you too. In those companies, it's almost a given that you have a PhD to do the research there – or a Master's with experience.

World-Renown

Another reason why people do PhDs is because they want to become world-renown. By publishing papers people will know their name. A PhD is not a shortcut to fame. To illustrate this point, tell us, how many people can you name with a PhD? How many scientists do you know of? If you're really good, you might be able to rattle off 100 names...but there are far more than 100 PhD holders and scientists that have lived. In the U.S. alone there are <u>currently</u> approximately 6 million PhD holders (yes, a 6 with 6 zeros behind it). So, a PhD isn't a shortcut to fame either. A fun fact: the person with the most citations in history is some called Michel Foucault. He has about 800,000 (that's about 799,500 more than a typical academic). Have you heard of him? Probably not...in fact, even most scientists can't really recall his name...

The more we discuss what a PhD will give you, the more you start to understand that, a PhD is what you make of it. It's not the title, but the skills that you learn through it, that will give you opportunities in the future. It's not the be-all and end-all, but a stepping-stone.

The skills and your thinking abilities that you develop over your PhD are well worth the time you'll have to spend on it, and the problems you'll face.

WHAT DO YOU DO DURING A PHD?

In a word, research.

It's succinct, but deceptively simple.

The act of doing research encompasses far more tasks than most people know, especially first-gens.

To illustrate how much you can unpack the word "research", let us give you a few questions.

You want to research, what are you researching?

Why are you researching that particular topic?

How are you researching?

With what money are you researching?

How are you going to disseminate this research?

These are just a few of the questions you need to answer if you want to research effectively. And a PhD teaches you how to answer all of these. If you learn the answers to these questions now, then your PhD will become much easier. Let's go through them one by one.

What Are You Researching?

We covered earlier how easy it is to be far too vague when trying to explain what you're researching. Even when you think you've given a precise and accurate explanation, it still could be very sloppy.

Let's go through another example to drive home how precise and accurate you must be when defining what you'll be researching.

Let's consider bees! Something so simple, yet, as you'll see, still complex enough to make you really think when developing a research aim.

Now, let's say you have a project, your project is to study the lifecycle of the bumblebee. Now, we've been so precise as to give the topic (the lifecycle) and also the particular species of bee (the bumblebee). What more could you want?!

We're no experts in bees, but just from that aim alone, several potential issues are glaring at us. For example, what do you mean by lifecycle? Is there one particular part of the lifecycle that you're studying, or the entire range? If it's the entire range, how will you be able to study their growth inside the egg? Or even earlier than that – while the egg is still inside the Queen? Will you study male or female bees? How will you tackle problems such as changes in temperature, rainfall, sun exposure? What about disease? How about the surroundings – do the number and types of flowers around the beehive make a difference?

So, you can see that we just touched the tip of the iceberg when it comes to defining what the topic is about, and already there are far more questions than we'd like to think about. But, that's the role of a researcher (and a PhD student): to have a topic so precise and accurate that not only people understand what you're researching, but you understand what you're researching. (That last bit is far more elusive than many people know – you'd be surprised how many PhD students are 2 or 3 years into their PhDs and they don't really know what their PhD is about!) Furthermore, if the topic were not well defined, then you'd be far less likely to use your resources and time as effectively as possible– you might use some resources to investigate the effects of sunlight on the lifespan of the bumblebee, while other resources are used on investigating the growth inside the egg; sure, they're probably related, but they're not really that close, as far as research questions go.

We've said a few times the words "precise" and "accurate" now. What do they mean? They're both very important when it comes to defining your research topic. So let's dive into them here.

Precise means that your topic needs to be very well defined, it must be very specific; taking the bee example, to make it precise, you'd cut away all of the variables except one or two very detailed ones, such as sunlight – you'd forget about flowers, rain, temperature, and so on, and just focus on the sun. Now, it's very likely that those other factors all affect the bumblebee's lifespan (and each other – for example, more rain could increase the number of flowers around the hive), but if there's no research focusing on the fundamentals, then it becomes increasingly difficult to ascertain the effects of even one of the factors on the lifespan if you try to investigate them all at the same time (you can do it, if you use statistics and a very well-thought-out research plan, but we won't go into that here). So, precise refers to cutting away all other potential avenues to investigate and defining one particular avenue in detail.

The word accurate refers to making the research topical – for example, if you defined your research project as, "investigate the effects of cow milk on bumblebee lifespan", it wouldn't make sense. Sure, it's fairly precise, but bumblebees don't drink cow milk, and as far as we know, cow milk and bumblebees don't really have anything to do with each other. So, the topic is just nonsensical. A far more accurate topic would be, "investigate the effects of a particular type of flower on the bumblebee lifespan" – we know that bees love flowers, and that pollen is an integral part of their lives, so that topic makes sense. It's an accurate topic.

Why Are You Researching
That Particular Topic?

This question is one of the most important questions; why are you researching the topic you're researching?

It is arguably more important than the topic itself. Let us explain.

As we covered, funding is critical for your PhD to go ahead. Without funding, it won't go anywhere. And as we said earlier, this funding comes from somewhere. In order to secure that funding, you have to justify to the potential funder why they should fund this topic of research. That's where the "why" comes into it. Why is the research important to begin with? In some very special cases, the funders don't care about the why, but 90% of the time they do. One special case is where the funder has had a very high revenue for a year and needs to get rid of some of the money to get tax breaks – enter your project.

The "why" of your project is also important purely from a project management point of view; what most people don't understand is that doing a PhD is an exercise in project management. You work on a project for years, planning it, making mistakes, fixing those mistakes, and so on. It is very good practice for a managerial role (despite many people not realizing that). The "why" of the project is very important for a project manager to know; they need to why they're doing a project in order to better direct the project. Here's an example to illustrate why: say you're developing a cleaning product and that's the only information you have. Your hands are incredibly tied because you don't know what features this product should have. Should it be non-toxic? You would probably immediately say yes, but it isn't necessarily the case; if the cleaning product were to be used in an industrial setting, then maybe toxicity isn't one of the most important features, but rather its cleaning ability is more important – you might have to tradeoff toxicity for cleaning power. On the other hand, if you're developing the product for the consumer market, then it almost certainly should be non-toxic. In other words, by knowing why you're doing something, you can better benchmark the importance of the various aspects of the project.

There's one more reason why the "why" of your project is important, and it's a much more immediate reason during your PhD; at some point (probably at many points) during your PhD, you'll have to explain why your research is important to someone. Chances are that that person will hold considerable power over the progress of your PhD. Clearly understanding the importance of your work and why it should be done makes it much easier to convince that person of the importance of your work. In other words, it will be much easier to convince that person to allow you to continue your work, or let you pass.

So, it's obvious that understanding, and being able to explain, why you're doing your work is very important. But, how do you figure that out? How do you figure out why you're researching a particular avenue?

That's where something called the "literature review" comes into play. You might have heard that term, you might not have. Let's go through it here briefly.

The literature review is exactly what it sounds like – it's a review of the literature. What does that mean though?!

Remember how we went through what papers were? Well, that's referred to as literature. What's more, any other document, such as patents, or even news articles and media releases, are considered part of the literature. The role of the literature review (often shortened to, lit review, or lit rev) is to succinctly sum up this body of knowledge. Once that body of knowledge has been summed up, the next task is to see what needs to be investigated next; by understanding what the current knowledge of the field is, you can then identify what should be investigated next. For example, let's go back to the bumblebee example (hope you like bees? ;)) ; say that you review the literature in the field to do with the lifespan of bees. You find that many other researchers have investigated the effects of various factors on the lifespan of bumblebees. The factors that have been covered so far include the sunlight, rain, temperature, various surrounding flowers, and certain diseases. These factors have been covered well in the literature. Now, the next step is to determine what you should investigate. By looking at the literature you now have a few options. 1) Pick a factor that hasn't been investigated yet. 2) Pick two or more of those factors already covered and investigate the synergy effects of them on the bees' lifespans (or you might even pick one factor that has been investigated already and one that hasn't). 3) Conclude that one of the factors already investigated wasn't investigated properly, so you will devise a better method to investigate it.

All of those options grow from the literature review; if you didn't do a literature review then you wouldn't be able to select the first option because you don't even know what's been done yet. You wouldn't be able to do the second option because you can't really determine the synergy effects without knowing the isolated effects of each factor. You wouldn't be able to do the third option because you wouldn't even be aware of the other investigations to begin with! So, you see how crucial a literature review is to your research?

By doing the literature review, you gain a lot more information about the "why" of your project. You nail down the reasons why you've selected the exact topic you did. As such, it becomes very easy to justify your research to others. The only thing left to do is to figure out why you should do that research at all? In other words, why is it even important to investigate factors affecting bumblebees' lifespans. The reason(s) why you should will usually come from the literature review as well; when you write a paper, in the introduction section, you usually have to discuss why the research field is important to begin with. Reading literature in your field will give you much of the justification why the field is important, so you don't really need to give it too much original thought (although, it is often wise to think about it yourself too).

(As a side note, if you want to read more about how to do a literature review, write papers, give presentations, and more, then we wrote another book just on those topics. It's called, "PhD 101: The Manual To Academia" by Dr John Hockey and Dr Sandeep Gupta. It's a little over 100 pages, and jam-packed.)

How Are You Researching?

This question is fairly straightforward, "how are your researching". That refers to the approach you're taking – what methodology are you using.

The method you use is incredibly important. For those in STEM, that's the main area in your research where weaknesses come from; yes, you can build weaknesses in from the lit rev and the conclusions you draw, but those weaknesses can be ironed out quite easily. The weaknesses built in through the method you use are far harder to iron out. The main reason is because you often don't see the weaknesses until you've already done your research. Catching weaknesses in your method BEFORE you carry out your research is far better than after. Nothing feels quite so deflating as when you realize there's a mistake in your methodology and you're now going to have a hard time extracting useful information from your results.

Make sure you analyze your method before you even start preparing your research campaign; the further along your research campaign you are, the worse a weakness in the method becomes – you can fix a weakness at the start before you've even begun gathering the tools and machines you need, it's way more difficult when you've already carried out the tests and you're now processing your data.

Let's see an example of that; let's return to our old friends, the bumblebees. Say that you were investigating the effects of one factor on their lifespans – the amount of sunlight for example. Well, the best thing to do is isolate that factor from everything else. That could be tough, but if you don't pin down the other effects, such as the surrounding flowers' influence, the influence of rainfall, etc., then it will be very difficult to say for sure what the effects of sunlight on the bumblebees' lifespans are. If you conduct your tests and afterwards you realize that you didn't take into account the effects of rainfall, then it might be almost impossible to determine. (As a side note, you might've realized that we said "almost impossible" in that last sentence. The reason why we said that is almost impossible is because after being in Academia so long, and having conducted so many research campaigns, we've learnt that you should never say that something is impossible – you might think it, and everyone might tell you it, but we've been surprised too many times to truly believe that anything is impossible. And that's the exciting thing about Academia, what you "knew" yesterday might be very different to what you "know" today. Cherish that, embrace that, and you'll become a far better researcher!)

The method you decide on using greatly impacts the findings you'll get, and the quality of those findings. Put effort into it from the beginning.

With What Money Are You Researching?

You might have noticed that we've talked about money quite a lot, and that's because it's what allows your research to happen. Without it you wouldn't have the equipment you need, or possibly even the supervision you need.

It's not only important because it determines what you can and can't do during your research (for example, you might only be able to afford a low-end machine that doesn't gather as much data as a high-end one), but it can also bias your research. We won't go into that because some people find it distressing and uncomfortable to think about.

How Are You Going To
Disseminate This Research?

Doing research without communicating it is usually pointless. It will be very rare to do research solely for yourself – even R&D companies that develop new products to sell need to have communication among the researchers, technicians, marketers, and managers. The same is true during your PhD; you'll have to communicate your work to a whole range of different people, from your supervisors, to your supervisory committee, to your department, to your fellow PhD students, to other researchers around the world, and to your funders.

The way in which you disseminate your research depends on the situation and your preferences. For example, conferences are very popular in Academia, they're where researchers meet and discuss their work. Usually at conferences, there are presentations given by researchers (and you'll probably give a few presentations during your PhD as well!) and other researchers sit and listen. There's usually question time at the end where the audience members can ask the presenter questions. But conferences are just one way of disseminating your research. Other ways include papers, patents, general chit-chat, and even online forums.

Doing research means to disseminate your work as well, through at least one channel. Many PhD students will see a large improvement in their communication skills during their PhDs, and you will too. So, don't get disheartened if your first draft isn't received well, or even if your 10th draft isn't, there are stories of papers taking years to be accepted and published – hopefully, you won't have any situations like that.

What Does The Day-To-Day Life
Of PhD Student Look Like?

We've covered that PhD students do research, and we've covered what "doing research" entails, but what does the day-to-day life of a PhD student look like?

Many people, even current students, wonder that. One of the reasons why current PhD students think about that is because they want to make sure that they're keeping up with everyone else. For those who only think about what the day-to-day life of a PhD student should be in order to make sure that they're keeping up, then the only thing they have to worry about is whether they're making progress on their project, not what everyone else is doing. That doesn't mean that they should be finishing their project, but simply making progress. It takes years to do a PhD, so don't expect to finish it in 6 months or even a year. Small steps lead to big achievements.

Others worry about what other PhD students are doing because they're worried that they're doing their PhD wrong. They try to look at what other PhD students are doing and copy them, much like you would during an exam when you look at your friend's paper and copy what they put down. If you haven't realized it yet, that tactic isn't very successful. First of all, there's no guarantee that your friend is doing it right, so you might be copying a wrong answer to begin with. Second, unlike an exam where every has the same questions and so copying gives you a decent chance of getting somewhere, everyone's PhD is different and so copying what your friend is doing won't actually help you in your PhD. Sure, there are certain checkpoints, like the lit rev and your dissertation, that everyone has, but the vast majority of your PhD will not follow anyone else's timeline. Some parts will seem to go slower than everyone else's PhDs, and some parts will go much quicker.

For those who are just genuinely curious about what the PhD life looks like, well it's not as glamorous as you might think. It's fairly mundane; some days will be just reading paper after paper for 8 hours. Other days will be preparing for your experiments/simulations. Other days will be planning your research, sourcing equipment, and figuring out how to stretch your resources to cover all your research planned. Other days will be filled with teaching and marking assignments (often PhD students will do some of the teaching and marking for their supervisor). Other days will be purely for writing, whether that's writing papers or even your dissertation – the further you get into your PhD, the more "writing days" you'll have. Other days will involve meetings with various people, from your supervisors to department chairs to even people in the media. And then there will be those days where you get those "Eureka" moments where you find the answers to your long-held research questions. Those days are probably the best – figuring out something that's been perplexing you for a couple of years is a great feeling.

Interspersed with all this are the frequent coffee breaks, the long and often random discussions with fellow PhD-students and lab-mates, and the obsessive hunt for conferences in dream-locations around the world (at least that's when COVID-19 isn't messing things up).

Unfortunately, because you're so focused on one thing for some many days in a row (your PhD question for upwards of 1,000 days), the days often blur together and many students have breakdowns. One way to combat this is to always look back at what you've done and think of the accomplishments you've had, even if they're small, like "understanding your field much better now", or "getting the machines in the lab to work".

The Milestones Of A PhD Project

While everyone PhD is different, there are certain milestones that almost all of them have. They include:

- The development of your research direction
- PhD confirmation
- Fulfilment of PhD requirements
- Dissertation submission
- Viva Voce/Defense

Everyone PhD will need to center around a particular focus. That focus derives directly from your literature review. Sometimes this isn't a formal milestone of your PhD, but sometimes you will need to write this focus down and log it with your university by a certain date. This might be 6 months into your PhD or even later.

PhD confirmation is the point in your PhD where you're effectively allowed to do the final tasks of your PhD; in most programs, when you enter, you'll be on some kind of probation. That could be 6 months, 1 year, or even longer. The convention is that people during this stage of the PhD process are "PhD <u>Students</u>". Then, you'll have your confirmation exam (also known as your candidacy exam). This is where you have to present your PhD project, your plan, any work you've done, and fulfil certain requirements by the university (for example, they might have a requirement that you need to have one paper submitted to a journal in order to pass). When you pass this exam, you're now called a "PhD <u>Candidate</u>". PhD candidates are usually in their last stages of their PhDs, but that doesn't mean that they're close to finishing yet – they often still need to carry out more research, write their dissertation, and pass their PhD Defense.

After the confirmation/candidacy exam, you then have to fulfil more requirements to write your dissertation and submit it. Once you've submitted your dissertation, one of two things usually happens. 1) your thesis is judged by your supervisory committee (a bunch of old academics judging your work for its merit). 2) you move straight onto your Defense. In the first case, you will get feedback on your dissertation before your Defense and you'll need to address those comments before progressing to the Defense. In the second option, the Defense and the dissertation corrections are all rolled into one major feedback at the end.

Now, what is a PhD Defense? (Also known as a Viva Voce). It's where you stand up in front of your supervisory committee (sometimes the general public can watch as well, but it depends on the university), and present your PhD work. They'll have copies of your dissertation, which you sent to them weeks earlier, in front of them with their notes and questions about your work. At the end of the presentation, they'll ask you questions about your dissertation and your presentation, and you'll have to "defend" your work. If you do it well, then you'll pass. But don't worry, usually the Defense is just for show, and unless you really screw up with ignorance or insolence, you'll pass.

IS BEING A FIRST GEN PHD'ER A DISADVANTAGE?

Now to the question that you probably came for.

Overall, it is harder for a first gen PhD'er than PhD students who have parents with PhDs. The main reason why is because you have to learn so much more. We've gone through many topics, such as research, papers, and citations, that non-first gen PhD students already have a strong handle on. As a first gen PhD student, you have to learn about these topics from scratch. But, you're reading this book, so you're getting up to speed and by the end of it, you'll be further along that even most non-first gens.

It's not all bad, though. In fact, first gen PhD students have some advantages. One of the major advantages is that you come into the academic environment with fresh eyes. You're not entering with preconceived notions about what to expect and what everything is. As a result, many of the strengths of Academia will stick out, but also, many of its weaknesses will also glare at you. For example, one of the weaknesses of Academia is one of the things that most people think is its strength – peer reviewing.

Peer reviewing is exactly what it sounds like, others in Academia (peers) assess your work (review). At almost every stage throughout your PhD, and academic life, there will be others assessing your work. For example, when you send your paper to a journal to get published, it will undergo a "peer review process". In essence, this is where a few people (who are hopefully knowledgeable in your field, but not always) will read your paper and give the journal and you feedback. This feedback goes a long way in determining whether your paper will be accepted. On the face of it, it's a great system. But two major problems arise. The first is a theoretical problem and the second is a practical problem.

The first problem is the peer review system itself; in essence, this system means that only ideas and work that are accepted by others will be put forward as fact. Well, what if you're smarter than everyone else? What if those assessing your work can't see the brilliance of it? These things happen more often than you'd think. And it's logical that they will happen. Think about it, if you're working on your niche topic for years then it makes sense that you're naturally going to be more knowledgeable about it than almost everyone else, so how are others going to be able to assess your work accurately if they don't know your niche field as well as you do? As a result of this mismatch in expertise, only research that the majority can understand will be held in high esteem, everything else will be seen as wrong. This means that breakthroughs almost never happen. The only time breakthroughs happen is when someone of very high standing in the academic community puts forward an idea, and everyone will naturally follow it because they automatically give it credit due to the high-standing of the person who put it through – it's a power-cycle. Because of this theoretical problem (which also exists in real life), the knowledge that Academia can find is inherently stunted.

The second problem that arises with the peer review process (now, we should mention that there are far more problems than just the two we're going through, but these are just examples) is that, while the peers reviewing your work should be experts in your field, in practice, this is not often the case; when your paper gets sent to a journal, the journal people then try to find people to review it. They usually try to get 3 reviewers (sometimes more, sometimes less). The problem is that getting 3 experts in your field to review your paper is difficult – academics have many things to do, and they can't dedicate so much time to peer reviewing research. They might review one paper a month (which is pretty good), but almost always the journal struggles to find 3 experts to review your work. Often, they'll find 1 or maybe 2. This has led to the joke about being "reviewer 2" – the idea being that, reviewer 2 is usually the worst reviewer because reviewer 1 is usually the expert, but then the journal struggles to someone just as good, and has to settle for someone who's kind of an expert, but not really, and these "kinda experts" usually overestimate their own knowledge and make life difficult for you. Finally, reviewer 3 is just some random person who doesn't know the field and doesn't even try to pretend to know it. As a result, reviewer 2 gives somewhat pertinent comments, but because of their lack of real understanding, the comments are often difficult and nonsensical. (A paper was published not long ago studying this phenomenon and it actually found that reviewer 3 is usually the worst, but the common joke in Academia is that it's still reviewer 2 who's the worst). So, the peer review process has problems with it from this practical standpoint – the simple logistical problem of finding people who are qualified to assess your work.

Being a first gen PhD student allows you to see these kinds of problems because you haven't inherited the views and opinions about Academia from your parents. Non-first gen PhD students usually have opinions and biases that they inherit from their parents and sometimes those opinions are objective and pragmatic, but other times they're warped and nonsensical. Coming in with fresh eyes is good if you're happy to see all the problems (and the strengths) inherent in Academia, but if you just want to get on with your work, then it can often be a distraction.

We'll move into the disadvantages of being a first gen PhD student, but before we do that, let's cover one last misconception.

It's true that first gen PhD students don't know as much about Academia as non-first gen students (generally speaking), but, often first gen PhD students don't realize that there are many things that non-first gen students don't know either. For example, it's very common for a first gen PhD student to feel like a fish out of water when they come across something they didn't even know existed (like the fact that you can get your dissertation published – if you didn't know that, then you'll know what I mean right now). <u>But</u>, the fact is that, many non-first gen PhD students won't know that you can get your dissertation published either. So, a first gen will often feel far more inadequate than they actually are because they don't realize that non-first gens are also on a learning curve and don't know everything either. They always assume that because they're a first gener, non-first gens will always know more than they do. This problem can become exacerbated when non-first gens try to hide that they didn't know something about Academia, or the PhD process.

Often, the feeling of being inadequate is far worse than the inadequacy itself, so if you ever do feel inadequate, just ask yourself this: "Why am I here? Is it because I already know everything, or is it because I don't and I'm here to learn?"

Obviously, you're there to learn, so to feel inadequate about not knowing something is illogical. What's more, many first gen PhD students (and PhD students in general), can't help but compare their PhDs with other PhD students. This is obviously setting yourself up to feel inadequate in some way because we often focus on negatives more than positives; you could be ahead in 10 different ways, but when you find one way in which you're lagging behind, you become fixated on it and feel inadequate". While this scenario might not seem funny to someone going through it, it is to someone who has finished their PhD. The reason is because trying to compare yourself to another PhD student is like trying to race someone else during an exam...except you don't have the same exam...or the same subject. What's more, you don't even know if they've done it right – they might've skipped half the questions on their exam, or just wrote anything down! So, how can you accurately compare when your works are completely different. This problem becomes worse when you try to copy the general work and tasks of other PhD students – "they're writing a paper, so I have to start writing one now!", "they're preparing for a conference, so I should go to a conference soon too!". Again, coming back to the idea of doing an exam, this is even worse because now it's like you're trying to copy someone during an exam...but you don't have the same questions, so you can definitely copy, but it won't make sense.

Let's move onto the disadvantages of being a first gen PhD student, and how to overcome them.

Perhaps the greatest disadvantage a first gen PhD student faces is doubt. Having a parent who has done a PhD and knows the general procedure greatly helps your confidence. You not only feel more confident because you come from a line of people who have done them before, but because those people provide feedback about your progress and can help steady any mood swings you have because of the work. What's more, you trust their judgement because they've been through it, so they know what you're going through. As a first gen PhD student, you don't have that peace of mind. You don't have that natural confidence because your parent hasn't done one, nor do you have someone whom you implicitly trust to steady mood swings. One common way to overcome this is to find a mentor, or even a support group. These people can give you advice and help settle down mood swings. The problem with this is that you usually don't know what the motives of the people giving you advice are, and you usually get what you pay for. Usually the only real way to overcome any lack of confidence is to develop a self-centered attitude. It might seem like a vice, but you're beginning to enter the real world – you're starting your career. It's called office politics. In most offices, the majority of the time and effort spent on work is well below 50%. Most of time and energy of the workers are spent trying to angle something better for themselves – it's self-centered. That's just how it is. Doing a PhD means that you're entering the workforce, whether you realize it or not; your supervisor, PI, professor, and everyone else employed at the university are <u>employees</u>. They're trying to build their careers, so you're part of the office politics whether you like it or not. With that, you simply need to adopt the right attitude and you'll be mentally fine. Be self-centered. That doesn't mean that you should never help anyone else, but when you do always make sure that you're not being put at a disadvantage, and it's even better if you can get some help from them in return.

We wrote about a lack of confidence being a disadvantage for first gens firstly because many of the problems that first gen PhD students (and PhD students in general) face stem directly from that lack of confidence. And it makes sense. For example, one of the most nerve-wrecking things any PhD student has to do is stand up in front of people and give a talk about their work. You not only have that fear of public speaking that so many people have, but you now have the added anxiety because you're laying your work on the line. You're opening your work, and yourself, up to anyone and everyone to criticize it. Those who are confident in their work don't have that problem. But as a PhD student, and a first gen one at that, you're often less confident in your work. There are a few tricks for overcoming that lack of confidence though. Let's go through them in order from most effective to least effective.

The first trick is to simply not care what others think. While this is the most effective way of dealing with a lack of confidence, it's also the hardest. The key to stop caring what others think is to trust in your work. Once again, that might seem helpful on the face of it, but how do you do that?! How do you stop your mind running wild with every doomsday scenario?! Simple! Read everything you can, think about every possible problem with your work, and prepare answers to those problems in advance. It's a lot of work to get to the stage where you're that well-versed in your research, but there are no shortcuts to hard work. And as a result, your work will be better and you won't be stressed out when showing other people your research. Let's go through that method a little more; at every step of your PhD, at every decision about your work, make sure that you think about all of the options. Make sure that you understand what each option will entail, how each option will affect your PhD, and how rigorous each one is. If you can't answer the following questions about each option, then stand back, think, ask around, and brainstorm until you can. These questions are:

- How does this option affect the quality of my work?
- What are the tradeoffs I need to make if I were to choose this option?
- Is this the best option?

Let's go through each of those questions.

What does, "How does this option affect the quality of my work?" mean? Let's go back to the bumble bee example. Say that you're investigating the effects of the sun on a bumble bee's lifespan. You could develop a whole raft of different methodologies to answer that question, but let's look at one specific choice you might need to consider; let's look at whether you'd use the real sun as the source of "sunlight" or an artificial light. When looking at each of these options you should ask, "how does this option affect the quality of my work?" Let's run through this question for each of the options we've highlighted (sunlight and artificial light). If you were to use real sunlight for your investigation, then some potential aspects that could affect the quality of your work include, what time of year you run your tests, where in the world you run the tests, in what type of weather you run your tests; if you run your tests in winter, then you're further away from the sun than in summer and the angle of the light hitting the earth at your location will be shallower, both of these facts mean that the sunlight will be less intense. That is obviously going to introduce questions into your work. Likewise, the location of the tests will greatly affect your results – not only will conducting them nearer the equator (or further north) will affect the intensity of the sunlight, but so will the levels of pollution. Furthermore, the weather could greatly affect your results – overcast days could block 5% of the sunlight, which could instantly introduce an error of 5% into your results.

Now, after briefly discussing those potential problems with using real sunlight, you might quickly jump over to wanting to use artificial light, but not so fast! Potential problems with artificial light can also be teased out; similarly, you would need to decide what spectrum to use and what intensity (do you want to mimic an equatorial location with high smog levels, or a very northerly location with very clear air?) What's more, you have to determine whether the artificial light you have has the entire light spectrum of the sun, both the infrared and ultraviolet components, and perhaps even more extreme than that.

Now, we've just gone through the first question, let's move onto the second question, "What are the tradeoffs I need to make if I were to choose this option?" Let's assume once again you have to decide whether to use real sunlight or artificial light for your tests. Each have their own advantages and disadvantages. Real sunlight is real, no one can say that there's something inaccurate about your sunlight – they might argue that it's only representative of very certain conditions, but they cannot say that it represents no conditions anywhere on earth – obviously it does at least represent the conditions you tested under! On the other hand, using artificial light will open your work up to criticisms about the "real-ness" of the light. Moving on, using real sunlight might make your experiments hard to carry out – you might have days where the lighting isn't what you want and you need to somehow factor the effects of undesirable lighting in to the results. On the other hand, using artificial light means that you'll have the exact conditions you plan for each and every day. Another tradeoff is, using good old fashioned sunlight means that you don't need to spend any money on fancy artificial lighting equipment, so it could be cheaper. That means that you could spend your funding elsewhere and improve other aspects of your work. So, you can see that your whole PhD work (and research in general) is one big tradeoff – at the very least, you'll be faced with decisions that will not only affect the quality of your current work, but also your future work.

Finally, for every decision you make, you need to run through each of the options and ask yourself, "Is this the best option to choose?" If, after going through the various ways each option affects the quality of your work, and the tradeoffs, you conclude that it is the best option, then congratulations, you're well on your way to being a very capable researcher! That's the aim of a PhD!

Reading all of these hard questions and potential problems might have you running in the other direction, it might make you think that doing a PhD isn't for you, but before you make your mind up just know that while you should do the exact same thing for every possible option you face in your PhD, it's not as hard as it may first seem – that's because the further your go into your PhD, the more your analytical skills will develop and running through potential problems like we just did will be second-nature, probably even first-nature. What's more, while many people dread having to make tradeoffs, it's actually a "get out of jail free card"; when you have to justify why you did something a particular way, you could always cite the fact that you had tradeoffs to make – perhaps you only had access to a particular type of equipment, or you were limited in the number of days you could spend on the work, etc. All of those tradeoffs and limitations are experienced by every researcher who has ever lived – no one has had access to unlimited funding or time – you can't spend $1,000,000,000 on one experiment and take 300 years to complete it. We all have limitations placed on our work. In order to be able to use this get out of jail free card (citing tradeoffs as reasons why your work is weak is certain areas), you have to have a coherent plan to your work. For example, if you spent your funding carelessly in the first couple of years of your PhD only to be left with nothing for the final years, then citing that you ran out of funding due to a lack of planning is not going to win anyone over. Conversely, if you deliberately planned to spend more on certain experiments than other, perhaps because those experiments were far more important than other ones you had coming up, then citing why you spent more on certain experiments (and as a result undermining the quality of other experiments) is completely justifiable. As long as you have a decent reason, then your research will be well received. The rare person you encounter who insists that everything should be perfect, and you should've spent all four years measuring the length of your shoelace to 1/1,000,000,000 of a millimeter, is out of touch with reality and you shouldn't worry about them because most researchers don't give those people's opinions any weight anyway. They're those people who most other researchers just roll their eyes at afterwards.

A final word about this way of overcoming a lack of confidence in your work; make notes about your decisions along the way. In your first couple of years, you might be able to cite off the top of your head why you chose to do something a certain way, but after 4 or 5 years, trying to remember back to why you made some of the decision you did in the first couple of years will be very tough. Having even rough notes about each decision will help greatly. Furthermore, try to organize those notes in a way that you can find them within 10 minutes of looking. Nothing is more humbling than finding the notes you needed 3 months after you needed them.

We've now covered the first trick, and the best way, to overcoming a lack of confidence.

The second trick to getting over a lack of confidence is to understand that research, and in particular science, is not that accurate; following on from the tradeoffs of the various light sources will make it clear that no method is perfect. What's more, what we knew yesterday could very well be different to what we know today, and what we know today could be different to what we know tomorrow; at one point in history the very notion that the sun was the center of the solar system was insanity! Everyone *knew* that the earth was center of the solar system and the universe! Anyone who espoused differently was a dummy.

Doing a PhD isn't about finding a universal truth that will stand the test of time – nothing does. A PhD is about doing research in an area to the current acceptable standard. One question that begs being asked is, "what is the current acceptable standard?"

The current acceptable standard is one that the majority of people with PhDs will accept as being adequately accurate. Let's unpack that sentence. We said the majority of people with PhDs – that doesn't mean that everyone will accept it, but many will. Almost every PhD student is afraid of professors because they assume that professors know far more about their work than they do. In some cases that is very true, but not always. Regardless, the point is moot because you're training to do a PhD, not to become a professor. So, if you present some work and a professor does point out a problem, then how is that such a bad thing? It took someone with a professorship to see that problem and you're not trying to get your professorship, you're trying to get a PhD. Anyone who tries to apply the level of competence required to be a professor to a PhD student is insane! It's like comparing a 10 year old's 3-mile running time with an Olympic runner's time! So, don't sweat it. All you have to aim for is what the majority of PhD holders will agree with.

The third best way of overcoming a lack of confidence in your PhD is to take up a hobby that you're good at. It can be anything from painting, to sports, to learning something new. Anything that gives you a sense of accomplishment will make you far more confident in your daily life and that will creep through to your PhD life as well. One of the big reasons why so many PhD students suffer breakdowns is because they make the initial mistake of letting their PhDs consume their whole lives. They cut away every other activity and hobby. As a result, their entire self-worth revolves around their PhD. That's a recipe for disaster because there are going to be good days and bad days. What you don't want is for your entire life to revolve around your PhD because then those bad days are going to hit much harder. So, make sure that you keep up your hobbies, and especially ones that you're good at. Those will give you a greater sense of accomplishment and make you more confident in general. They'll balance out those bad days.

The fourth way of overcoming a lack of confidence is therapy. One great thing about the recent past is that therapy is not really a dirty word anymore. Going to therapy no longer brands you as unstable, and it's becoming quite common for people from all walks of life to get therapy. So, if it helps you, then all the more power to you. The reason why we've put this method as the fourth best way of getting over your lack of confidence is simply because most therapists don't know what you're going through. There's a big difference between knowing what someone is going through by hearing about it, and knowing what some is going through because you've been through it yourself. And that's really the simple reason why therapy is not that useful. If you have other problems in your life that creep through, then therapy might be a good option because the therapist might have a lot of experience with those other problems, but if the underlying reason for you lack of confidence is specifically due to a PhD-related aspect, then therapists will usually be ineffective.

Scholarships

One of the greatest problems that most PhD students face, not just first gen ones, is a lack of money to live. Some PhD programs will give you a nice salary, but others will leave you literally having to do odd-jobs to make ends meet.

However, one caveat to being a PhD student is that there are many scholarships out there, and many of them don't have very strict requirements. For example, if you're studying Chemistry, then there are many scholarships by various organizations to help PhD students who are doing Chemistry. Some scholarships are literally open to everyone, everywhere, and every subject. What's more, there are scholarships for all sorts of categories, from women in STEM (women who are doing PhDs in Science, Technology, Engineering, or Mathematics), to even those who are first gen PhD students. There are many scholarships available and they range from tens of thousands of dollars for each year of your PhD to a few hundred dollars as a one-off payment. Make sure that you trawl the internet, get in contact with unions at your university, and even just ask around to find as many possible scholarships as you can. From there, make sure that you apply – you'd be surprised how many scholarships are actually very easy to get simply because there's almost no competition; because most PhD students don't look around for scholarships, they never apply and that means that you could literally be the only one who has applied for a particular scholarship. Barring any factor making you ineligible, the odds of you getting a scholarship where you're the only one who applied is 100%, just in case you weren't clear about what we're getting at ;) . We even heard recently of one scholarship fund begging people to apply because they had literally no one applying for it – not because it was a bad scholarship but simply because no one knew about it.

A final word about scholarships, if you're already getting some kind of scholarship from your university, then you should make sure with them that you can receive additional scholarships from elsewhere. Some universities don't allow it, but others do. It's as simple as emailing the HR (Human Resources) people and asking. Even if you're not allowed to hold another scholarship, then that shouldn't prevent you from applying to other scholarships because they might be bigger, and in the event that you're successful, you might be allowed to drop your university scholarship and take the bigger one – just check to make sure that that's alright with your university first (again, through the HR people). As a side note, the HR people might also have some leads for scholarship opportunities as well.

Where are some places to find scholarship? Many people think that it's hard to find scholarships, after all, it seems logical that it shouldn't be easy – why would someone want to give away money? But the reality is that there are a whole host of ways to find scholarship opportunities, and they're actually more accessible than you'd think, if only you spend some time looking for them. Obviously, the general internet is great, but you could also ask other PhD students, various university admin staff (including the HR people), and even on social media; for example, on Twitter, there are whole accounts dedicated to simply finding scholarship opportunities and retweeting them to their followers. So, just spend a few hours looking, then a few more applying, and you might be much better off soon – no more eating ramen 14 times a week, or sitting outside the coffeeshop to use their free internet.

First Gen Stigma

Being a first gen PhD student is starting to come with its own stigma. A couple of decades ago, there wasn't even a distinction between a PhD student who was a first gen and one who wasn't. Nowadays, that distinction is becoming sharper and sharper. What does that mean?

It means that, as we briefly discussed earlier, many people will see you as being less proficient in PhD studies to begin with. They'll see you as someone who has to learn a little more. That will inevitably translate into a longer timeframe to do your PhD than someone who isn't a first gen. It will also translate into a lower chance of getting into a PhD program. But as we've also covered briefly, the belief that a first gen isn't as good at PhD work as a non-first gen at the start isn't entirely true. Sure, a student who has at least one parent with a PhD will be more familiar with academic lingo, which will often make them more confident because they feel slightly better off than first gen students. But with confidence often comes complacency. Your proficiency in academic work is not the only thing that will determine how successful you are. Your attitude is equally important.

I (John) wrote about the importance of attitude in another PhD book ("PhD Imposter Syndrome; Stopping It Dead In Its Tracks"), but from a different angle. We want to revisit the importance of attitude, but from the angle of a first gen perspective.

We've all come across people who are naturally gifted in certain things. And while most of them shine in the short term, long term they actually do worse than most others. Let's have a look at an example; when I (John) was doing my PhD, I had a friend who was naturally smart. We had known each other for years even before doing our PhDs.

When we first met, he was just starting to get a reputation for being very intelligent. He was getting the best grades. As the years wore on, his reputation for being intelligent grew, but so did his complacency. You see, that reputation was his prison. The longer it went on, the more he got sucked into it. And the more he got sucked into it, the more precious it became and finally it reached a point where he couldn't stand being seen as not the most naturally gifted person in the room. The problem was that we still had exams and tests, and so on. He realized that it was not always certain that he would get the best mark – naturally, there will be others who excel at certain things. The chances of him being better at everything than everyone were tiny. He knew this. So, to combat this and preserve his reputation of being the most naturally gifted person *ever* he adopted the only logical approach to preserve his "naturally gifted" façade. He started to slack off. His reasoning was that, if he could get good grades (not the best, but good) but with almost no effort, then obviously he was still the most naturally gifted because if he did apply himself, then he'd probably get the top mark.

So, you see how a reputation can become a prison and actually lead you to underperforming?

Let's pursue this example further, because we still have many more years to cover with his case – and fortunately because he was a good friend of mine, I had front-row seats the entire time. We entered our PhDs around about the same time and we enjoyed the new reputations of being smart enough to get into PhD programs. For me, that reputation was neither here nor there – I never really cared much about what people thought of me because I instinctively knew that whatever they saw was only a mere fraction of who I was. He, on the other hand, had carried through his unbridled fondness of his reputation of being naturally gifted (I should also mention at this point that he was not a first gen student, but many around him were. In those days, no one held the fact that you were a first gen against you – it didn't matter from a political point of view, which gives us a unique chance to see just how important the effects of being a first gen are when you take out all stigmas. In fact, the term "first gen" didn't even exist yet).

My friend's troubles only worsened during his PhD. He now had such a fragile reputation that he felt so pinned down by it and he almost flat-out refused to work. He'd do a couple hours a week on his PhD. His peers were doing upwards of 40 hours a week. The years wore on and he slowly relinquished his hardened belief that he didn't need to work – whether he ever believed that or not is questionable, but he definitely kept that façade up to anyone around him. Because I knew him so well, I could read his facial expressions very well and I could tell when things weren't as pleasant as he'd make them out to be.

Finally, he caved and had to work around the clock to finish his PhD.

A few things happened, and being an outside observer allowed me to see them all. For him, his vision was clouded by his emotions, let me explain.

When he caved and finally decided to work his tail off, in his mind his reputation shattered – he had been holding onto the reputation of being naturally gifted, and his work ethic had molded to it so strongly, that when he finally had to work, in his mind the entire reputation became invalid. As a result, even though he got his

PhD, on graduation day his face was something similar to how I would imagine a bank robber's face would be while being interrogated by Batman. In other words, he felt so undeserving of it that his face displayed terror and shame.

That was one of the things that had happened. As I said, to him that was the only thing because he was so caught up with his old reputation that nothing else really mattered. But, two more very important things happened. The first was his PhD was very weak in the end – he hadn't put in the hard work over years, only at the end, and it was quite obvious. While it still met the criteria of his university to be awarded a PhD, his PhD quality was definitely on the lower side. That made it rather difficult for him to get a job straight out of his PhD. He finally got a job, but not long after, it kind of disintegrated around him – that was largely due to the fact that he didn't develop as much as he should have during his PhD, and that was because he simply was terrified of putting in the effort.

The second important thing that happened (which he didn't realize) was that, after his reputation shattered, no one cared. The ironic thing was that his reputation mattered far more to him than it did to anyone else, and as the years went by that divide became greater, and that happens to everyone. You see, when you first start your PhD, you might be used to having quite a lot of time on your hands – let's face it, Bachelor's and Master's degrees are pretty easy (if you don't think so, then just wait until you're doing your PhD, then you'll see what we mean) and you're often left with quite a lot of time. Much of that time is spent socializing, and with that socializing comes a greater importance you place on how people see you and how you see others. At the start of your PhD, you might still carry this type of thinking through, but by the end of your PhD, you simply don't have time to care what other people think, let alone care what you think of other people. Reputations don't really matter, you're just doing your work with your head down. So when my old friend ended up caving and actually working, no one even noticed much. And to tell you the truth, if it weren't for his facial expressions during that period, I probably wouldn't have noticed either. The funny thing was that he never realized that this whole sequence of events went largely unnoticed, he never realized that no one cared, or even took much notice. So after his PhD, he slowly fell back into his old habit of slacking off and exaggerating how naturally gifted he was, thereby re-plastering the walls of his old prison and making them just as strong as ever, maybe even stronger.

Let's bring this back to the idea of first gen versus non-first gen. There are some key similarities between my old friend (who actually was a non-first gen, back in the days before the terms even existed) and current non-first gens; they both have a reputation of being ahead of the pack simply due to luck, and they know it. Furthermore, the more the idea that being a first-gen is a disadvantage takes hold, the more superior a non-first gen will feel, which will make them even more similar to my old friend. The more a non-first gen gets caught up in their image of being naturally gifted, the less capable they'll become because their attitude will hold them back from actually working.

What does that all mean? It means that, currently, non-first gens have an advantage simply because they have more general knowledge about Academia, but the more they're touted as being naturally gifted, and as such more capable than first gens, the less capable they'll become because if their egos are continually played to, their natural advantage will not be enough to overcome their reluctance to work, and first gens will become more capable. So, everyone who tries to argue that first gens are at a disadvantage are actually making the overall situation more advantageous for first gens because non-first gens begin to slack off. The only caveat is for you not to buy into the idea that you'll always be at a disadvantage.

HOW TO START

Once you get accepted into your PhD program, you'll be faced with the unenviable challenge of deciding how to start.

If you're lucky, you'll have great supervisors who will guide you closely and instruct you every step of the way until you're comfortable and capable of doing it yourself. You should note that this would be the ideal situation for <u>every</u> PhD student, not just first gens. In reality though, supervisors who do that are rare, and they're rare for a number of reasons.

Supervisors often have many other tasks to do, they might have other PhD students to supervise, or grants to apply for, or lectures to give, and so on. While that shouldn't stop them from giving you the guidance you need, in reality it often does. You might also get unlucky and get supervisors who don't really pay their students too much attention, and that could be simply because they don't want to or because they've had so many students over the years that they become complacent supervisors (it happens!). And finally, you might just get terrible supervisors – we don't want to get into that too much here because we've written extensively about how to deal with terrible supervisors in past. What we will do in this book is give you an idea of how to tell if a supervisor will be good or not.

To determine whether a supervisor will be good or not, do the following:

- Observe how happy their current students are
- Observe whether their past students still talk with them, and if so, how is the relationship
- Ask them how many hours per week their students work to be successful

If you do all of these things and you find any of the following then you should try to find another supervisor (preferably before you even start):

- The students are miserable
- The students don't like their supervisor
- The students aren't doing very well or are behind schedule
- Their past students don't talk with them, or if they do their relationship is very strained
- You'll be expected to work long hours, for example 60 a week

Assuming that you're not one of the lucky ones who gets the "supervisor of the year", how should you start your research?

Two words: "literature review".

You've almost certainly done a literature review before, but despite that, you'd be surprised how many people don't really know what a literature review is for and why it is arguably the most important part of your research – we know, right! How could doing a literature review, where you're not actually doing any original research, be the most important part of your work?!? Before reading on, ask yourself what a literature review is for. Take 10 minutes to really tease out the answer. We've covered it earlier in the book, but we're just trying to it cemented in your mind.

Have you done that?

Okay, good, let's discuss what a literature review is, what it's for, and why it's so important. We've already covered this earlier as well, but it is so important that we should briefly cover it again, especially because this will be your first step in your research.

Simply put, a literature review is a review of the literature. You read everything (or as much as you can) about your particular field. If you're lucky, the exact topic you'll be researching has been determined before you start and you can simply download all the papers on that exact topic and read. If you're in the situation where your each niche hasn't been determined for you, then that's okay because you get a little more freedom to select what you want to research, but unfortunately at the beginning it means that you need to read a lot more, simply because you need to read as many papers as possible on the general field to get an idea of a good niche area to concentrate on.

So, what you do is read all you can find on your subject. You should make notes about each paper (you can find a literature review note template at https://www.johnhockey.university, as well as many other resources to make your PhD easier, for free):

-       What the general topic was

- What the specific topic was
- What method they used
- What their findings were
- When the paper was written
- What weaknesses in the research were there
- What future directions for the work were given, or can be inferred

Once you've done that, then you're ready to write your literature review.

Now, the literature review is crucial for a few reasons. The first is to get an idea of the field, what's been done, what hasn't been done, and why. The next reason is to give you a good idea of potential avenues to research. The final reason is to make sure that you don't do anything that has already been done, or is currently underway with another research group.

The reason why you don't want to do something someone else has done is because PhDs are all about original research. If you do something that someone else has done, then that will severely undermine your chances of passing. The only time when it is acceptable to knowingly do something that someone else has done is to make sure that the results are repeatable. Just a heads up, they rarely are – that's called "The Reproducibility Crisis". The main reason why results are rarely repeatable is because not all the factors are the same among labs. What's more, it's rare for the person carrying out the research to fully appreciate all the factors that affect their results.

So, the very first step to doing your PhD, other than getting your office organized, is to search for all the literature on your topic. Once you have it, read it. That part might take you 3 months, so don't worry if all you seem to be doing day in day out is reading for the first few months, it's normal! Remember to make notes while you read. After that, get your notes and start writing your literature review.

Remember, the aim of your literature review is to arrive at a point where you've identified a worthwhile avenue to research.

Let's unpack that word, "worthwhile". What does that mean? It means a few things. The first one is that there will be enough there to make a PhD out of. Unfortunately, you're almost never going to know how much you need to make a PhD – you're new and you've never done one! That's what your supervisors are there for. Another thing that worthwhile means is that, the research is actually important enough to conduct – that means that it either adds value to society (directly or indirectly) or can generate profits for the university or a company, or both!

Doing this part of your PhD properly will take up the first 3-6 months. After that, it's time to start building a plan for your work. Building accurate plans are hard. Especially if you've never done a PhD before. But, if you sit down and think pragmatically about your work, what it will entail, what resources you have, and what you're aiming for, you can build a fairly accurate plan. It's simply a case of being methodical and identifying what the pressure points are. By identifying what the pressure points of your work are (those points that everything hinges on), you can better support them and ensure that you get over any problems with them. For example, one pressure point could be that you need a particular machine to do your research. If you don't have that machine or access to one, then you need to figure out how to get one. If you can't, then you need to find a workaround. That might mean that you need to adopt a different methodology, or it might even mean that you need to slightly change the focus of your research. It happens!

A final word about building your plan, whatever timeframe you come up with, multiply it by a factor of 2-4; depending on the person, it might only take you 2x as long as you expect. Whereas other people might take up to 4x as long. The more practiced you become at making plans for your research, the smaller that factor will become.

So let's see an example about how to plan with that factor included. We just said that a literature review can commonly take 6 months. But let's break down the workload to get an idea of the timeframe.

Say you need to do the following tasks in order to do your literature review:

- Download all literature on your subject
- Read all of the literature and make notes
- Go over the notes and think deeper about your field
- Write your literature
- Arrive at a precise and accurate aim for your PhD research

So, downloading all the literature; at the beginning, you'll be able to find the bulk of the literature on your field, but as you keep on reading, here and there papers might pop up. So, at first you might find 100 papers on your field, then after reading all of those papers, you might have another 20 that pop up. So, as you keep on reading, you'll be downloading here and there. Overall, the download process to find and get 120 papers might take 1 week.

Reading all of the literature, let's say 120 papers will be: 120 papers / 4 papers per day (assuming you're able to read 4 papers a day) = 40 working days. Assuming that you work 5 days a week, then that's 8 weeks. You could add another couple of weeks to that for miscellaneous tasks, like making notes, meetings, and general distractions. So, let's say in total 10 weeks for this part. Note that this would be a very thorough literature review.

Now, going over your notes and actually writing might take only 2 weeks.

Tallying all of this up will give you approximately 13 weeks. 3 months. You could double this estimate, and you'd get 6 months. And that's a perfectly reasonable timeframe. Why would you double it? Because things might pop up that you didn't expect – maybe you need to take a day here or there to learn about the lab, or teach, or mark assignments, etc. Or maybe you'll actually find 150 papers or even 200 papers instead of the assumed 120 papers. Or maybe your writing will take longer than you expected.

By working in a decent factor, like 2, you give yourself a much better estimate because it's impossible to take into account <u>every-thing</u> that could go wrong when you're planning. So, the factor takes care of that.

As we said, a literature review that covers 120 papers is quite thorough, on average; some fields might only have 30 papers, and others might have 300.

After you've done your literature review and plan for your work, you should be around about 8 months into your PhD. From here, you'll probably start "the real work" of actually carrying out research. What's more, once you're at this stage, almost every disadvantage in the knowledge of the PhD process a first gen has compared to a non-first gen will be non-existent. The only disadvantage that remains is the lack of someone who has done a PhD steadying your emotional swings that you might have during your PhD. That's the topic of the next section.

HOW TO KNOW IF YOU'LL FINISH

Being a first gen means that you lack the support of someone close to you, who knows intimately about the PhD process, who can give you encouragement. Sure, you might have family and friends who will encourage you, but sometimes it is little consolation simply because they don't really know. They're just offering moral support but that support doesn't have the knowledge to back it up.

That uncertainty can be debilitating for first gens. That's one advantage that many non-first gens have. So, how do you steady your emotions when things seem to be going wrong, when you don't have anyone around who can really console you?

There are many different problems you could face during your PhD. It could be that your research isn't working out the way it was planned. It could be that you're locked in a political battle with your supervisors. It could be that you've run out of funding. And so on. We've also written books on many different problems and how to overcome them – the exact methods to use, when, and why, but we cannot go through them here as whole books are required for those subjects, and those topics are often not solely experienced by first gens.

Instead, there's one key thing that all solutions to every problem you might face have in common: Never give up.

Unfortunately, that phrase has been used so much over the years that it has become somewhat meaningless to those who have never experienced its power. So, let's go through why never giving up is important. Why never giving up will lead to a solution.

There's a solution to everything. You just need to find it. When you've tried everything, and nothing has worked, then the thing that you haven't tried will be the solution. What's more, when you feel like all hope is gone and you want to give up, then that is precisely the time when you should not give up because that is the time when sticking with it will have the greatest effect.

Think of it this way, every problem has a solution. The only difficulty that arises is knowing what the solution is. So, logically, all you have to do is go through every possible idea and eventually you'll find the solution! It's really that straightforward. Never giving up will mean that sooner or later you'll come across the solution. The only thing you need to consider is whether you have the time for it. However, time is often misunderstood – how many times have you estimated how long something will take and been wrong? Probably every time you do something. Even if you've driven from home to the university 10,000 times, you will almost never get the exact travel time right. The same is true with every time estimate you make. So, don't be disheartened if you think something will take a billion years to figure out, because often all it takes is one "eureka" moment and that estimate of a billion years drops to a couple of weeks. That's the funny thing about trying to estimate how long it will take to solve a problem, you're trying to estimate how long it will take to find the solution but you don't know what the solution will be. So, how could that time estimate ever be right?! It's like going prospecting for gold and saying, "I'll find a huge nugget in two weeks". How do you know? Sure, you might find one, but you'll never know the timeframe because you haven't found it yet!

Moral of the story is, never give up. Even if you think it will take forever to solve the problem, you'll likely be wrong about that time estimate. Keep at it and eventually you'll find the solution. And you might find it sooner than you expect!

CONCLUSION

Being a first gen PhD student has a growing stigma of being inherently at a disadvantage. That disadvantage comes about directly through not having learnt what Academia is, what the various important areas of research are, and what research is to begin with! You haven't grown up in that environment, so that creates that lack of understanding. But, in most cases the perceived disadvantage is much greater than the actual disadvantage.

We went through a few factors that can exacerbate the discrepancy between the actual disadvantage you have to the perceived disadvantage. Some of those factors included, how continually touting that non-first gens have an advantage will naturally lead them to becoming more complacent, and that non-first gens don't understand everything about Academia anyway.

Many first gens don't understand how the academic system works from what professors do, to how research works, to what the role of PhD students are in the university, and so on. That knowledge is one of two major obstacles in a first gen's way. Fortunately, we covered all of these aspects, so you now know how a university works and the role of these positions in it. You also know how a university can be divided into two main halves. The first is the dissemination of knowledge and the second is research.

We went further and explained the underlying premise of Academia – your peers reviewing your work. We also highlighted the major theoretical and practical problems with this system, but also highlighted how this system works and how you fit into it.

Next, we went through how to start your PhD. You have the first 8 months' worth of work already laid out ahead of you to simply follow. That's a huge advantage over every other PhD student because even non-first gens typically enter their PhDs and don't have a clear idea about how best to start. They need to rely on their supervisors to tell them, which is exactly what a typical first gen student also has to do. But, you're now ahead of the game.

Finally, we tackled the second major disadvantage that a first gen PhD student faces – not have adequate moral support. Non-first gen students are naturally confident that they'll finish, at least more confident than first gens. However, we broke done logically why you don't need moral support to finish – sure, it would be nice, but that card isn't in your deck. Alternatively, by rationally thinking about the situation, you can determine that you will eventually finish. As long as you don't give up, then it is almost a certainty that you'll finish. And guess what, that's the only thing that non-first gen PhD student gets from their parents, a simple belief that they'll finish. But, you don't need to get that belief from someone when it's obvious how just sticking through with your PhD will sooner or later lead to success.

AFTERWORD

We hope you liked the book. If you have any questions about it, you can reach us a number of different ways, from through John's website (https://www.johnhockey.university), to on Twitter (@JohnHockey18), to email (thephdcommunity@gmail.com), or even through Amazon.

We're always happy to interact with PhD students and help them out.

If you're new to your PhD and want step by step instructions on how to write the various documents (lit review, papers, etc.) of your PhD, understand how to give a great academic presentation, as well as understand all the different metrics to measure academic (and PhD) success by, then check out one of our other books, "PhD 101: The Manual To Academia". It picks up where this one finishes and is good for both first gens and non-first gens. You can find it here (https://johnhockey.university/product/phd-101-the-manual-to-academia-ebook-edition/).

Another book we wrote that is highly suited to PhD students just starting out (both first gens and non-first gens) is, "How To Get Your PhD: How To Set Your PhD Up For Success In The First 12 Months". It goes through the political side of your PhD and outlines how the work you do is usually not important to getting a PhD, and how the politics usually overrides it. It also outlines what you need to do to make sure that you succeed. You can find it here (https://johnhockey.university/product/how-to-get-a-phd-how-to-set-your-phd-up-for-success-in-the-first-12-months-ebook-edition/).

Other books by the author(s) include

Cheats and Walkthroughs

https://johnhockey.university/product/phd-cheats-and-walkthroughs-ebook-edition/

Doing A PhD Being A Woman!

https://www.amazon.com/PhD-Woman-Doing-Being-ebook/dp/B082YGYFVD/ref=sr_1_1?dchild=1&keywords=doing+a+phd+being+a+woman&qid=1595576924&s=digital-text&sr=1-1

PhD Imposter Syndrome: Stopping It Dead In Its Tracks!

https://www.amazon.com/PhD-Imposter-Syndrome-Stopping-
Tracks-ebook/dp/B083ZD917L/ref=sr_1_1?
dchild=1&keywords=imposter+syndrome+stopping+it+dead
+in+its+tracks&qid=1595577012&sr=8-1

The PhD Student's Guide To Processing And Presenting Important
Data

https://johnhockey.university/product/phd-guide-processing-
data/

Do You Want Your PhD Now? The PhD Student's Stratagem

https://johnhockey.university/product/problems-with-phd-
supervisors/

Should You Do A PhD? The Ultimate Guide

https://www.amazon.com/Should-You-Do-PhD-Ultimate-ebook/dp/B087QQWBX4/ref=sr_1_1?
dchild=1&keywords=should+you+do+a+phd+the+ultimate+guide&qid=1595577062&sr=8-1

The "John Hockey" Method For Coaching PhD Students"

https://johnhockey.university/product/john-hockey-coach-phd-students/

All of these books are available as Ebooks and Paperbacks. For the paperbacks, you can order them through Amazon.

Made in the USA
Middletown, DE
02 March 2021

34618188R00061